SHORT CIRC

WALKS

around

HARROGATE

by
John N. Merrill

Photographs and Maps by John N. Merrill

FOOTPRINT PRESS Ltd.,

1997

Short Circular
Walks Series.

"from footprint
to finished book."

FOOTPRINT PRESS Ltd.,
19, Moseley Street,
Ripley
Derbyshire
DE5 3DA
Tel/Fax 01773 - 512143

View from Sierra Blanca over White Mountains

Printed, bound, marketed and distributed by Footprint Press Ltd.

© Text and routes - Suncrest Ventures Ltd.1997.
@ Maps & photographs - Suncrest Ventures Ltd. 1997.

First Published   -April 1992.
Reprinted 1995 and 1996.
This edition - March 1997

ISBN 1 874754 80 6

Please note - The maps in this guide are purely illustrative. You are encouraged to use the appropriate 1:25,000 O.S. map.

Meticulous research has been undertaken to ensure that this publication is highly accurate at the time of going to press. The publishers, however, cannot be held responsible for alterations, errors, omissions, or for changes in details given. They would welcome information to help keep the book up to date.

British Library Cataloguing-in-Publication Data. A catalogue record of this book is available from the British Library.

Typeset in Bookman - bold, italic and plain 9pt and 18pt.

Designed and typset by Suncrest Ventures Ltd.

Cover © Suncrest Ventures Ltd.

CONTENTS

About John N. Merrill

John combines the characteristics and strength of a mountain climber with the stamina and athletic capabilities of a marathon runner. In this respect he is unique and has to his credit a whole string of remarkable long walks. He is without question the world's leading marathon walker.

Over the last twenty-five years he has walked more than 160,000 miles and successfully completed more than a dozen walks of a least 1,000 miles or more. His six major walks in Great Britain are -

Hebridean Journey....... 1,003 miles.
Northern Isles Journey......913 miles.
Irish Island Journey ....1,578 miles.
Parkland Journey.......2,043 miles.
Land's End to John o' Groats.....1,608 miles.

and in 1978 he became the first person to walk the entire coastline of Britain - 6,824 miles in ten months.

In Europe he has walked across Austria - 712 miles - hiked the Tour of Mont Blanc, completed High Level Routes in the Dolomites and Italian Alps, walked the Normandy coast, the Sentier de Seine (200 miles) and the Loire Valley (450 miles) in France, and the GR20 route across Corsica in training! Climbed the Tatra Mountains, walked in the Black Forest. and climbed all the highest mountains and skied in Norway 8 times. He has walked across Europe - 2,806 miles in 107 days - crossing seven countries, the Swiss and French Alps and the complete Pyrennean chain - the hardest and longest mountain walk in Europe, with more than 600,000 feet of ascent!

In America he used The Appalachian Trail - 2,200 miles - as a training walk, before walking from Mexico to Canada via the Pacific Crest Trail in record time - 118 days for 2,700 miles. Recently he walked most of the Continental Divide Trail and much of New Mexico; his second home. In Canada he has walked the Rideau Trail - Kingston to Ottowa - 220 miles and The Bruce Trail - Tobermory to Niagara Falls - 460 miles.

John set off from Virginia Beach on the Atlantic coast, and walked 4,226 miles without a rest day, across the width of America to Santa Cruz and San Francisco on the Pacific coast. His walk is unquestionably his greatest achievement, being, in modern history, the longest, hardest crossing of the U.S.A. in the shortest time - under six months (178 days). The direct distance is 2,800 miles.

Between major walks John is out training in his own area - The Peak District National Park. He has walked all of our National Trails many times - The Cleveland Way thirteen times and The Pennine Way four times in a year! He has been trekking in the Himalayas five times. He created more than a dozen challenge walks which have been used to raise more than £500,000 for charity. From his own walks he has raised over £110,000. He is author of more than one hundred and twenty walking guides which he prints and publishes himself, His book sales are in excess of 3 million, He has created many long distance walks including The Limey Way , The Peakland Way, White and Dark Peak Challenge walk, The Rivers' Way, Belvoir Witches Challenge Walk, The Sweet Pea Walk and Middlewich Challenge.

INTRODUCTION

This selection of walks is a little self indulgent. I spent ten years in boarding schools - 5 years in Harrogate and 5 years in Wetherby. The latter school, which alas is defunct, was revolutionary for its time and had it been operating today would still be way ahead of its time. In essence the co-educational boarding school was run on Quaker lines but the pupils had a major say in the running and operation of the school. Not only did we have the usual school cirriculum but we maintained the gardens, the vegetable/fruit area, the woodlands, the building of our own sewerage plant etc. In fact outdoor work was a major ingredient to the schools success. We all had different tasks each week in squads such as washing up duties, peeling potatoes, coal shifting etc. In many ways a bit like an extended Outward Bound course, but one that really prepared you for life. I personally owe the school and headmaster a great debt for setting me on my way in life and work.

On Saturday afternoons and all day Sunday you were free to do what you liked. On Sunday's you could go to the kitchen and make your own sandwiches and disappear for the day, writing where you have gone on the blackboard; so long as you were back for evening assembly. Most Sunday's I was off on my bike and I would cycle to the main "outdoor" recreation areas - to Brimham Rocks, Almscliffe, Plumpton Rocks, Fountains Abbey etc. During the summer we had weekend camps near Patley Bridge. As a result I have very fond memories of the area - yes, for me, my school days were a very happy time.

The walks in this book have returned me to my favourite haunts, but this time on foot to enjoy even more their setting and beauty. I derived much pleasure from exploring again the area I was "brought up in", and hope you too come to enjoy this area of "land between the parks", for it has much to offer.

Happy walking!
John N. Merrill. 1997

Ripon Canal and River Ure - Bishop Monkton walk.

Footbridge in Cardale Wood - Beaver Dyke Reservoir walk.

ABOUT THE WALKS

Whilst every care is taken detailing and describing the walk in this book, it should be borne in mind that the countryside changes by the seasons and the work of man. I have described the walk to the best of my ability, detailing what I have found on the walk in the way of stiles and signs. Obviously with the passage of time stiles become broken or replaced by a ladder stile or even a small gate. Signs too have a habit of being broken or pushed over. All the route follow rights of way and only on rare occasions will you have to overcome obstacles in its path, such as a barbed wire fence or electric fence. On rare occasions rights of way are rerouted and these ammendments are included in the next edition.

The seasons bring occasional problems whilst out walking which should also be borne in mind. In the height of summer paths become overgrown and you will have to fight your way through in a few places. In low lying areas the fields are often full of crops, and although the pathline goes straight across it may be more practical to walk round the field edge to get to the next stile or gate. In summer the ground is generally dry but in autumn and winter, especially because of our climate, the surface can be decidedly wet and slippery; sometimes even gluttonous mud!

These comments are part of countryside walking which help to make your walk more interesting or briefly frustrating. Standing in a farmyard up to your ankles in mud might not be funny at the time but upon reflection was one of the highlights of the walk!

The mileage for each walk is based on three calculations -

1. pedometer reading.
2. the route map measured on the map.
3. the time I took for the walk.

I believe the figure stated for each walk to be very accurate but we all walk differently and not always in a straight line! The time allowed for each walk is on the generous side and does not include pub stops etc. The figure is based on the fact that on average a person walks 2 1/2 miles an hours but less in hilly terrain.

7

BISHOP MONKTON
& RIPON CANAL - 4 1/2 MILES

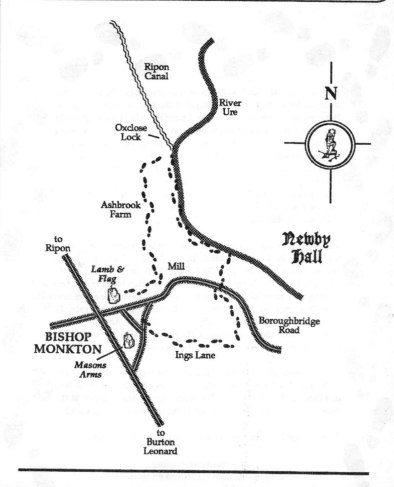

RIPON CANAL - Authorised in 1767 and completed in 1773, made part of the River Ure navigable from the River Swale via Boroughbridge to Ripon. The canal section is 2 1/4 miles long from Oxclose Lock to Ripon.

NEWBY HALL - Started in 1705 by Sir Edward Blackett. In the mid 18th century, the new owner, William Weddell, had the house redesigned and enlarged by Robert Adam. As a result the building is Adam's finest; open to the public.

BISHOP MONKTON & RIPON CANAL
- 4 1/2 MILES
- allow 1 1/2 hours.

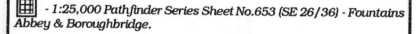

- *1:25,000 Pathfinder Series Sheet No.653 (SE 26/36) - Fountains Abbey & Boroughbridge.*

- *Bishop Monkton - Ashbrook Farm - Oxclose Lock, Ripon Canal - River Ure - Boroughbridge Road - Ings Lane - Bishop Monkton.*

 - *No official one.*

- *Masons Arms and the Lamb & Flag in Bishop Monkton.*

ABOUT THE WALK - Quite simply a stunner! Bishop Monkton is a very attractive village with stream running through it. The Ripon Canal is short but in a stunning location. You only see the start of it from the River Ure. A walk along the river gives you views of Newby Hall before returning along a track - Ings Lane - back to Bishop Monkton. I had the walk to myself and saw numerous birds including -grey heron, coot, mallard, curlew, oystercatcher, and a kingfisher! I throughly enjoyed this walk and hope you do as well.

WALKING INSTRUCTIONS - Walk along "Main Street" (Boroughbridge Road) past the Mechanical Institute and Post Office on your right. A few yards later at Fern House turn left, as footpath signed, and walk along the track towards Ashbrook Farm. Walk past the farm on its lefthand side to a gate. Keep the hedge on your left and at the end of the field reach a stile. After this the path is a track for a short distance to a field corner. Here keep the hedge on your right and descend gently to a stile and Oxclose Lock is just ahead. Walk to the lock and the Ripon Canal before turning right and walking along the banks of the River Ure with views of Newby Hall. After 1/2 mile cross a footbridge and less than 1/4 mile later turn right at a stile, and walk beside a stream on your right. After more than 1/4 mile the path emerges by a path sign onto the drive of a house on your right. Turn left to the Boroughbridge road. Turn left along the road for approximately 100 yards to a gate and pathsign on you right. Go through this and keep the hedge on your right to a stile. Soon afterwards is another and here you gain the hedged track which you follow all the way back to Bishop Monkton. After 1/4 the track turns sharp right and a further 3/4 mile you enter Bishop Monkton opposite the Masons Arms. Turn right along the Main Street.

FOUNTAINS ABBEY - 4 1/2 MILES

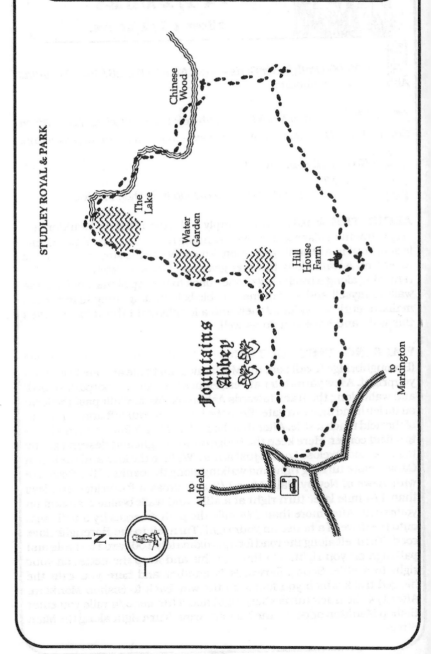

FOUNTAINS ABBEY
- 4 1/2 MILES
- allow 1 1/2 hours plus time for exploring the abbey

O.S. MAP - 1:25,000 Pathfinder Series Sheet No. 653 (SE 26/36) - Fountains Abbey & Boroughbridge.

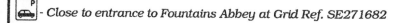 - Car Park - Fountains Lane - Abbey Wall - Hill House Farm - Mackershaw Trough - River Skell - The Lake - Fountains Abbey - Car Park.

P - Close to entrance to Fountains Abbey at Grid Ref. SE271682

☕ Tearooms at northern entrance to Fountains Abbey.

ABOUT THE WALK - This is an expensive walk as you will have to pay to park your car at the abbey car park, but this is refunded - taken into account - when you pay your entrance charge to Fountains Abbey - National Trust property. The walk though is outstanding past the largest monastic ruin in Britain and through a most attractive dale through which the River Skell meanders. You walk anti-clockwise on purpose to see from above the setting of the abbey before walking through it with time to explore and appreciate the monastic accomplishments and impressive water gardens of Studley Park.

WALKING INSTRUCTIONS - Turn right out of the car park and ascend the road to the road junction and turn left along the Harrogate Road - "Fountains Lane". On your left is the Abbey wall. Follow the road for 1/4 mile to a public bridlepath sign on your left. Leave the road here and follow the defined track with the remains of the Abbey wall on your right. You soon have impressive views down onto the abbey on your left. Continue to the righthand corner of a wood where there is a gate. Beyond follow the track down and round to the right to Hill House Farm. The path basically keeps to the righthand side of the farm and is well footpath signed. Go through a gate and continue on a track and descend to a wood and gate. The well defined path keeps just inside the wood and over the wall on your left you may see the herd of red deer. Keep in the wood for 1/2 mile and descend to a track in shallow valley.

Here turn sharp left and descend the track still in woodland to a footbridge, on your left, over the River Skell. Turn left and follow the well defined path along the dale floor crossing numerous footbridges and in 3/4 mile gain The Lake. Continue around the righthand side of it to the tearoom and entrance to Fountains Abbey. Having paid your entry fee walk into the abbey grounds either walking on the lefthand side or righthand side of the valley; either way will bring you past the impressive water gardens to abbey. Continue past the museum and Fountains Hall to the road and the car park is opposite to your left.

FOUNTAINS ABBEY - was founded by Cistercian Monks in 1132 and is the largest monastic ruin in Britain. The adjoining Studley Royal, also National Trust property, contains 18th century landscaped gardens with the abbey forming a magnificent backdrop. Fountains Hall dates from the 1560's.

Remember and observe the Country Code

 Enjoy the countryside and respect its life and work.

 Guard against all risk of fire.

 Fasten all gates.

 Keep your dogs under close control.

 Keep to public paths across farmland.

 Use gates and stiles to cross fences, hedges and walls.

 Leave livestock, crops and machinery alone.

 Take your litter home - pack it in; pack it out.

 Help to keep all water clean.

 Protect wildlife, plants and trees.

 Take special care on country roads

 Make no unnecessary noise.

RIPLEY PARK
& CASTLE - 4 1/2 MILES

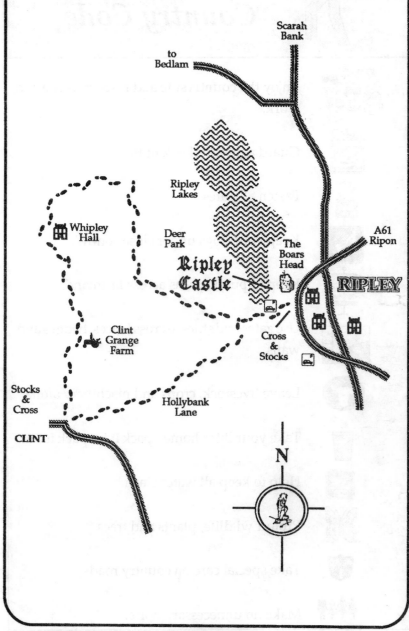

Scarah
Bank

to
Bedlam

Ripley
Lakes

Whipley
Hall

Deer
Park

Ripley
Castle

The
Boars
Head

A61
Ripon

RIPLEY

Clint
Grange
Farm

Cross
&
Stocks

Stocks
&
Cross

Hollybank
Lane

CLINT

N

RIPLEY PARK & CASTLE
- 4 1/2 MILES
- allow 1 1/2 to 2 hours.

O.S. MAP - *1:25,000 Pathfinder Series Sheet No.653 (SE 26/36) - Fountains Abbey & Boroughbridge.*
- 1:25,000 Pathfinder Series Sheet No. 663 (SE 25/35) - Harrogate.

- *Ripley - Hollybank Lane - Clint - Clint Grange Farm - Whipley Hall - Deb Well - High Rails Farm - Park Lodge - Sadler Carr - Ripley.*

P *- Beside the walls of Ripley Castle or at the southern end of the village at Grid Ref. 284604.*

- The Boars Head, Ripley.

ABOUT THE WALK - A walk full of history - Ripley Castle, Ripley stocks and cross and in the churchyard a weeping cross. In Clint is another cross and stocks. You return around Ripley Park and no doubt catching sight of the deer that roam there, before seeing once again the lakes with Ripley Castle behind.

WALKING INSTRUCTIONS - From the cross and stocks in the cobbled square in Ripley, walk down past the church the on your left and castle on the right into Hollybank Lane - part of the Nidderdale Way. The track descends to a footbridge over Ripley Beck, with impressive waterfall from the lake. Continue round on the track and in 1/4 mile it divides. The one to your right is the one you will be returning on. Keep to the lefthand one, still Hollybank Lane, and walk through Hollybank Wood to a lane. Keep ahead on the lane to its junction nearly 1/2 mile later at the hamlet of Clint. Here you turn right infront of Clint Cottage, along the track to Clint Grange Farm. But before doing so it is well worth just walking ahead a short distance to see the cross stump and stocks of Clint.

Follow the track to Clint Grange Farm and turn left at a gate and shortly afterwards go through another. Cross the field aiming for the righthand side of a small wood, where there is a stile. Keep the wood on your right around the field to a gate on your right. Go through this and keep the field boundary on your left - a fence - to another gate and into Whipley Hall. Here turn left and follow the lane around to your right. Where it forks take the lefthand one and in a few yards, just after a lefthand bend is a recess in the hedge on your right where Deb Well is and a stile. Over the stile keep straight ahead to a small plantation where there is a stile. Walk through to another stile. Here turn right on a track which ascends to the perimeter wall of Ripley Park, and a kissing gate. Through this continue beside the wall on your left to another kissing gate. Soon afterwards gain the track from High Rails Farm. Turn left along the track, still keeping the boundary wall of Ripley Park on your left. Pass Park Lodge and in another 1/2 mile reach Hollybank Lane, you walked along earlier. Turn left along it and retrace your steps back to Ripley.

RIPLEY - The church, dedicated to All Saints, was rebuilt in the late 14th century. Inside is a 14th century effigy to Sir Thomas de Ingilby, whose family owned the castle. The weeping cross in the churchyard is said to be the only one in the country. The base has eight niches in it, for kneeling while you repent. It is believed to date from the 2nd century. The castle is open on Sundays and the gate house dates from the 15th century. The main hall dates from the 18th century. The Library has the foundation charter for Mount Grace Priory, near Osmotherley, which is seen from The Cleveland Way.

Ripley Castle.

THE HIKER'S CODE

✿ Hike only along marked routes - do not leave the trail.

✿ Use stiles to climb fences; close gates.

✿ Camp only in designated campsites.

✿ Carry a light-weight stove.

✿ Leave the trail cleaner than you found it.

✿ Leave flowers and plants for others to enjoy.

✿ Keep dogs on a leash.

✿ Protect and do not disturb wildlife.

✿ Use the trail at your own risk.

✿ Leave only your thanks and footprints - take nothing but photographs.

BRIMHAM ROCKS
- 7 1/2 MILES

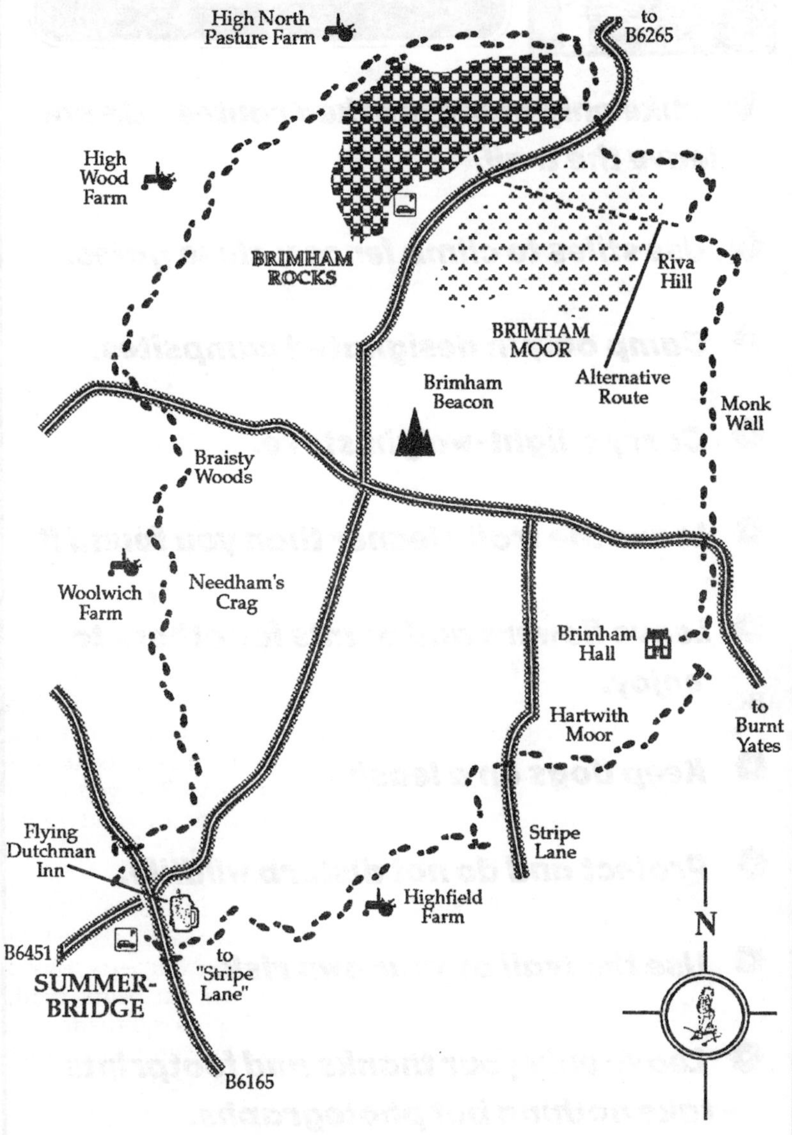

High North Pasture Farm

to B6265

High Wood Farm

BRIMHAM ROCKS

Riva Hill

BRIMHAM MOOR

Brimham Beacon

Alternative Route

Monk Wall

Braisty Woods

Woolwich Farm

Needham's Crag

Brimham Hall

Hartwith Moor

to Burnt Yates

Flying Dutchman Inn

Stripe Lane

Highfield Farm

B6451

SUMMER-BRIDGE

to "Stripe Lane"

B6165

N

BRIMHAM ROCKS
- 7 1/2 MILES
- allow 2 1/2 hours.
- longer if exploring the rocks.

O.S. MAP - *1;25,000 Pathfinder Series Sheet No. 653 (SE26/36) - Fountains Abbey & Boroughbridge.*

- Summerbridge - Highfield Farm - Hartwith Moor - Brimham Hall - Monk Wall - Riva Hill - Brimham Moor - Brimham Rocks - High North Pasture Farm - High Wood Farm - Braisty Woods - Woolwich Farm - Old Spring Wood - Summerbridge.

- roadside parking in Summerbridge, on B6165 road just south of Flying Dutchman Inn. National Trust parking at Brimham Rocks.

- Flying Dutchman Inn, Summerbridge.

ABOUT THE WALK - Another of my haunts! I spent many a summer's day exploring these incredible gritstone rock formations; sometimes by cycling here at other times walking from a campsite near Pateley Bridge. My aim was to encircle the rocks so that you could admire them in their setting while exploring more of the area and seeing other rock formations.

WALKING INSTRUCTIONS - From the Flying Dutchman Inn in Summerbridge walk southwards along the B6165 road (to Ripley). At the end of the houses on your left turn left, as footpath signed - "Stripe Lane" - and ascend The Whinfields. The path soon bears right, following a track to a farm which you walk round on its righthand side and ascending to a gate. Continue ascending to the righthand corner of the field where there is a stone stile. Continue to another stile and a track. Keep ahead on the track to another by a footpath sign. Cross over to a stile and keep the field boundary on your right before curving round to your right to Highfield Farm. Walk through the farm and upto

Moor Road. Turn left along the road and in 1/4 mile leave it at a stile on your right - at the end on the second field on your right. Keep the wall on your right as you descend to a stile. Here aim for the righthand side of Brimham Hall where there is a gate. Walk through the farm and upto a minor road.

Here turn left and in a few yards where it turns left keep straight ahead on a public bridleway, part of the Nidderdale Way. The track is beside the Monk Wall on your right. To your left can be seen the large gritstone tower known as Brimham Beacon. After 1/2 mile at a footpath sign keep left on the track with Riva Hill on your left. In little more than 1/4 mile reach the perimeter of the National Trust property of Brimham Rocks. Go through the gate and after a few yards turn right and walk along the righthand side of Brimham Moor, close to the wall on your right. In theory there should be a right of way across the moor but on the ground it does not exist. A path does exist close to the wall. After more than 1/2 mile reach a track and turn left along this to the minor road across the moor.

You can as an alternative, rather than walk along the wall side of the moor, continue ahead to the road and into Brimham Rocks. Here you explore the rocks and on the northern side of the trig point 301m. is a right of way down to a stile and track close to High Pasture Farm. Here you rejoin the main route by turning left.

Gaining the moor road turn right along it and follow it for 1/2 mile to a righthand corner, here turn left onto a track, which in 1/2 mile leads to High North Pasture Farm. Where it turns right to the farm keep straight ahead to a gate, the other side of which is the stile and path from the trig point. Cross the field to a stile near the far righthand corner of the field. Keep the wall on your left to a gate and enter woodland. For the remainder of the walk you are heading southwards to Summerbridge. Walk through the wood to a stile. Then across the field to a gate and onto the lefthand side of High Wood Farm where there is a gate. Keep to the left of the farm and cross the next field to a ladder stile followed by a stile. Here bear right and keep the wall on your right as you curve round to another stile and cross a small stream. Continue ahead to the immediate right of a wood where there is a stile. Keep the wood on your left to gain another stile and track. Cross this and keep the wall on your right to another stile and on across another field to a gate in the lefthand corner.

Here gain a minor road and turn left then right at a stile and footpath sign. Cross the field to a stile and enter the righthand edge of Braisty Wood. Keep the wall on your right and gain a track. Here bear left along it and pass Woolwich Farm. Continue along the edge of the woodland

and passing Needham's Crag on your left and enter Old Spring Wood. About a 1/3 mile from the farm you approach a small building in the wood. A little before it turn right to a stile and descend by a wall to a drive and descend this to the road in Summerbridge. Turn left to the Flying Dutchman's Inn.

Brimham Rocks.

River Nidd bridge - Knaresborough walk.

KNARESBOROUGH
& THE RIVER NIDD
- 4 1/2 MILES

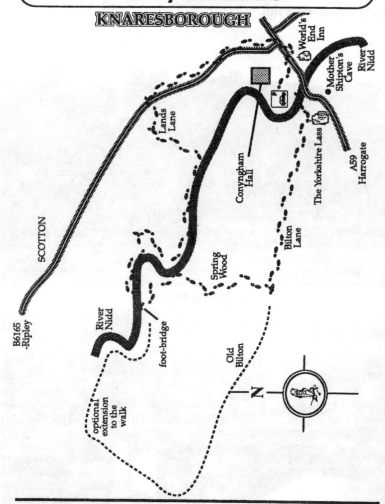

KNARESBOROUGH

World's End Inn

Mother Shipton's Cave

River Nidd

The Yorkshire Lass

A59 Harrogate

Lands Lane

Conyngham Hall

Bilton Lane

SCOTTON

Spring Wood

B6165 -Ripley

River Nidd

foot-bridge

Old Bilton

optional extension to the walk

N

KNARESBOROUGH - Well worth exploring and full of interesting buildings, including a ruined 14th century Castle, a museum with armour worn in the battle of Marston Moor, the oldest Chemist shop in England, and a Manor House; you can visit Mother Shipton's Cave, a woman of the 16th century for forecast motorcars and planes; or you could go boating!

KNARESBOROUGH & THE RIVER NIDD
- 4 1/2 MILES
- allow 1 1/2 to 2 hours.

- 1:25,000 Pathfinder Series Sheet No. 663 (SE 25/35) - Harrogate.

- Conyngham Hall Car Park (Knaresborough) - Ripley Road (B6165) - River Nidd - Footbridge - Spring Wood - Bilton Lane - Conyngham Hall Car Park.

- Conyngham Hall, opposite Mother Shipton"s Cave.

- Numerous in Knaresborough but passed en route are - The World's End at the start! and The Yorkshire Lass at the end.

ABOUT THE WALK - The River Nidd is particularly attractive on the western side of Knaresborough, being a wooded gorge. This walk takes around part of it. It is possible to extend the walk by 1 1/2 miles and explore more of the river and walk through Old Bilton village, which has an inn!

WALKING INSTRUCTIONS - Return to the road from the car park and ascend towards the town. After 1/4 mile turn left along the Ripley Road (B6165), along High Bond End. Keep on this road for 1/2 mile to the second road on your left - Lands Lane. Turn left along it, as footpath signed - "Nidd Gorge". Follow the road round to your right and by Beech Cottage turn left, as path signed - "Nidd Gorge", and descend to the river. The path is well defined and keeps close to the river on your left. After 3/4 mile you ascend away from the river to avoid a rocky outcrop, before descending, back to the river. Shortly afterwards reach the footbridge and cross over.

The main route now turns left but by turning right you can extend the walk by 1 1/2 miles. First you walk along the riverbank for a mile before ascending a track to Old Bilton village. Here turn left through the village and keep ahead on a track joining the main route back to Knaresborough.

Over the bridge turn left and keep close to the river for a short distance before ascending steps away from it. Continue on the path through Spring Wood, keeping close to its edge. In time you join a track, still close to the wood, and 1/2 mile from the river gain Bilton Lane. Turn left along the track passing Bilton Wells and Bilton Hall on your left. Keep straight ahead and gradually descend back to the river and road opposite Mother Shipton's Cave and beside the Yorkshire Lass Inn. Turn left across the bridge and left back into the car park.

BIRK CRAG
AND BEAVER DYKE
RESERVOIRS - 8 MILES

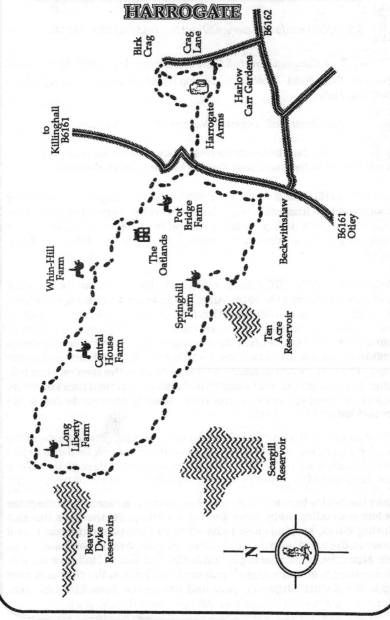

HARROGATE

B6162

Birk Crag

Crag Lane

Harlow Carr Gardens

Harrogate Arms

to Killinghall B6161

Pot Bridge Farm

Beckwithshaw

B6161 Otley

Whin-Hill Farm

The Oatlands

Springhill Farm

Ten Acre Reservoir

Central House Farm

Scargill Reservoir

Long Liberty Farm

Beaver Dyke Reservoirs

N

BIRK CRAG
AND
BEAVER DYKE
RESERVOIRS
- 8 MILES
- allow 3 hours.

 1:25,000 Pathfinder Series Sheet No. 663 (SE25/35) - Harrogate.

- Crag Lane (Harlow) - Birk Crag - Cardale Woodland - Pot Bridge Farm - The Outlands - Whin-Hill Farm - Central House Farm - Long Liberty Farm - Beaver Dyke Reservoirs - Springhill Farm - Beckwithshaw - Cardale Woodland - Crag Lane.

 - No official one.

- Harrogate Arms, Harlow. Another is just off the route in Beckwithshaw.

ABOUT THE WALK - Birk Crag was just down the road from my Harrogate school - Grosvenor House School on Duchy Road. The crag was one of those places that initiated me into the world of outdoors and cemented my love of walking and exploring the countryside. The walk begins from Crag Lane and takes you to the western edge of the crag before crossing the high country to Beaver Dyke Reservoirs. Here you cross to the otherside of the valley and pass rock formations and views to the Cleveland hills as you return to Crag Lane. You walk a small section of the starting out path twice and most of the route is along well defined tracks. If time permits you can explore more around Beaver Dyke Reservoir - adding a mile to the walk, by walking to Haverah Park Top and back from Long Liberty Farm.

WALKING INSTRUCTIONS - Starting from Crag Lane at Harlow, walk along the lane pass the gardens to its end close to Birk Crag. On the crag turn left, as signposted, and follow the path over the rocks and through woodland before bearing left to a beck and footbridge. Cross over and gaining the track bear right - footpath signed "Pot Bank". You will walk along the track to your left to the Harrogate Arms, at the end of the walk. Follow the track through Cardale Woodland to the B6161 road. The section from the footbridge to here you will do at the end.

Turn right and descend the road and cross the road bridge over Oak Beck. A short distance later turn left along the farm road past Pot Bridge Farm. Continue along the farm road to The Outlands. Here keep to the right of the farm to a gate. Continue along a track with woodland on your left to another gate. Turn left to another and keep the stone wall on your right as you walk along the field boundary for 1/2 mile to Whin-Hill Farm - the route is well stiled and gated.

Gaining the farm drive continue ahead, heading due west, first past Prospect House on your left, then through the middle of Central House Farm. The way now becomes a walled track for just over 1/4 mile, before becoming just a track with a wall on your right. 1 1/2 miles from Central House Farm gain the footpath junction and farm drive to the right of Long Liberty Farm. Here turn left and descend to a gate and and footpath sign. If you turn right at the path sign you can explore Beaver Dyke Reservoirs. Go through the gate and descend the field to a gate and water authority road. Turn left along the track/road and in 150 yards just before a cattle grid, turn left and ascend to a ladder stile. Cross the next field diagonally, using the electricity poles as a guide and reach a gate. Go through this and continue on a track and pass the ruins of a farm on your right after 1/4 mile. Follow the track round to your right and keep the wall on your right as you cross the country to Springhill Farm over 1/2 mile away. On your right can be seen a small rock outcrop and Ten Acre Reservoir.

At the farm gain a good track and follow it to your right then left around a small wood. Keep on the track for more than a mile to the B6161 road opposite the cricket field, just north of Beckwithshaw. Turn left along the road; to your right is an inn in Beckwithshaw. Descend the road back to the path you used in the early stages of the walk and turn right along it. Retrace your steps along the track to above the footbridge. Keep on the track to the Harrogate Arms and turn left up the drive to Crag Lane. Turn right to your start.

Beaver Dyke Reservoir.

EQUIPMENT NOTES

.. some personal thoughts from John N. Merrill

BOOTS - For summer use and day walking I wear lightweight boots. For high mountains and longer trips I prefer a good quality boot with a full leather upper, of medium weight, with a vibram sole. I always add a foam cushioned insole to help cushion the base of my feet.

SOCKS - I generally wear two thick pairs as this helps minimise blisters. The inner pair are of loop stitch variety and approximately 80% wool. - Thorlo socks are excellent. The outer are a thick rib pair of approximately 80% wool.

WATERPROOFS - for general walking I wear a T shirt or cotton shirt with a cotton wind jacket on top. You generate heat as you walk and I prefer to layer my clothes to avoid getting too hot. Depending on the season will dictate how many layers you wear. In soft rain I just use my wind jacket for I know it quickly dries out. In heavy or consistant rain I slip on a neoprene lined cagoule, and although hot and clammy it does keep me reasonably dry. Only in extreme conditions will I don overtrousers, much preferring to get wet and feel comfortable. I never wear gaiters!

FOOD - as I walk I carry bars of chocolate, for they provide instant energy and are light to carry. In winter a flask of hot coffee is welcome. I never carry water and find no hardship from not doing so, but this is a personal matter! From experience I find the more I drink the more I want and sweat. You should always carry some extra food such as trail mix & candy bars etc., for emergencies.

RUCKSACKS - for day walking I use a climbing rucksack of about 40 litre capacity and although it leaves excess space it does mean that the sac is well padded, with an internal frame and padded shoulder straps. Inside apart from the basics for one day in winter I carry gloves, balaclava, spare pullover and a pair of socks.

MAP & COMPASS - when I am walking I always have the relevant map - preferably 1:25,000 scale - open in my hand. This enables me to constantly check that I am walking the right way. In case of bad weather I carry a compass, which once mastered gives you complete confidence in thick cloud or mist.

PLUMPTON ROCKS
- 6 1/2 MILES

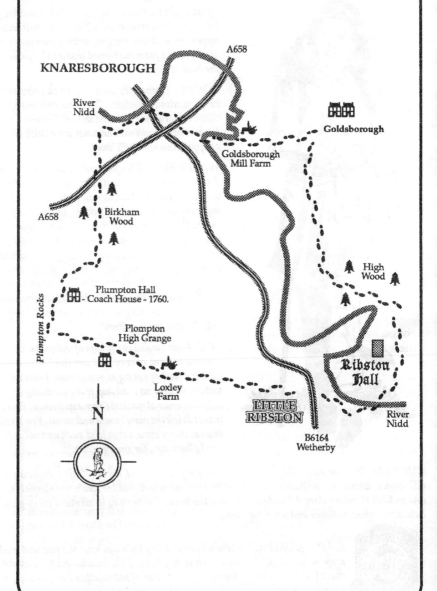

KNARESBOROUGH

A658

River Nidd

Goldsborough

Goldsborough Mill Farm

Birkham Wood

A658

High Wood

Plumpton Rocks

Plumpton Hall
- Coach House - 1760.

Plompton High Grange

Ribston Hall

Loxley Farm

LITTLE RIBSTON

River Nidd

N

B6164 Wetherby

PLUMPTON ROCKS
- 6 1/2 MILES

- allow 2 1/2 hours.

 1:25,000 Pathfinder Series Sheet No. 663 (SE 25/35) - Harrogate.

⚫⚫ ₌⚫ ⚫⚫ *- Little Ribston - Loxley Farm - Plompton High Grange - Plumpton Hall - (Plumpton Rocks) - Birkham Wood - Goldsborough Mill Farm - Mill Road - High Wood - Ribston Park - Little Ribston.*

 - No official one.

- None on the walk - sorry! Nearest at Goldsborough 1/4 mile from route.

ABOUT THE WALK - Plumpton Rocks was another of my favourite haunts and one a cycled to frequently. They are usually open at weekends during the summer. As a result I wanted to explore the area more fully and the impressive Ribston Hall came as a surprise. The rocks are set in a wooded vale with a lake and the weathered gritstone shapes are worth exploring if time permits. Little over half-way round the walk you walk above the River Nidd and have views to Knaresborough.

WALKING INSTRUCTIONS - Starting from Little Ribston walk to the northern end of the village to a footpath sign on your left near Holly Cottage - your return route comes in from your right. Follow the track round to a gate and continue on the track with the hedge on your right. At the end of the large field bear right then left and cross a footbridge keeping the hedge on your left, now. Gaining the edge of Braham Wood bear right along a concrete track through it towards Loxley Farm, which you pass on the lefthand side. Continue on a track to Plompton High Grange, which you pass on your right. Continue on a concrete track to a junction by a path sign. By walking to your left you will reach the entrance to Plumpton Rocks. Turn right and pass the Coach House of Plumpton Hall, dated 1760. Keep on this well defined track and follow it round to your right to Birkham Wood. Here turn left and walk just inside the wood on the track/path and cross the A658 road. Continue and in a 50 yards bear right keeping to the perimeter of the woodland and soon walking above the River Nidd. Continue beyond the wood and walk through a caravan site with views of the river and Knaresborough. Continue to the road junction of the A658 and B6164 road.

Cross over, as bridlepath signed and walk across the bridge over the River Nidd. To your left can be seen Goldsborough Mill and where the mill wheel was. Follow the well defined track - Mill Road - round to your right and in more than 1/2 mile gain the outskirts of Goldsborough. If you keep ahead you will come to the inn. Turn right along the tarmaced lane and follow it for a mile to its end, where there is a footpath sign. Continue ahead with the field hedge on your right to a bridge. Cross this and continue on the track to a gate on the edge of High Wood. Go through and follow the track round to your right to another gate and then a stile. The path bears left along the edge of the grounds of Ribston Hall before reaching the drive, which you follow to your right to the lodge, gates and bridge over the River Nidd. Keep on the drive and in 1/4 mile where it leaves the river side leave it to a stile on your right. Cross the field towards the far righthand corner, but before you get there, there is a stone stile on your right in the wall. Over this walk down into Little Ribston to where you began.

River Nidd and Goldsborough Mill.

Almscliffe Crag.

Clint - Stocks and cross - Ripley Castle & Park walk.

ALMSCLIFFE CRAG - 3 MILES

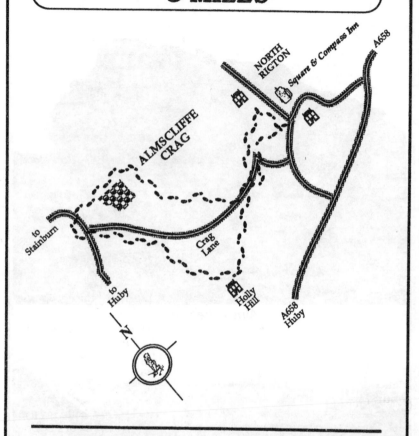

Turn left and left again past Crag Farm on your right. 50 yards later pass Cliff House and turn right immediately down to a stile and footpath sign. Cross diagonally to another stile and descend the next field to a stile and on to another. Here bear left along the hedge on your left to a stile with woodland on the right.Continue ahead beside the woodland to Holly Hill. Turn left to a stile by a lamp post and cross to another. The pathline now gently ascends diagonally to your right, and is well stiled. After five fields and stiles you reach Crag Lane by the footpath sign - "Huby" - and turn right. In a few yards on your left is your earlier path to Almscliffe Crag. Just after is the one to North Rigton. Don't take it but go straight across to another which is fenced and on the immediate left of the houses. Follow it round to Brackenwell Lane. Here turn left and left again to return to the road junction beside the Square and Compass Inn.

ALMSCLIFFE CRAG
- 3 MILES
- allow just over an hour.

 1:25,000 Pathfinder Series Sheet No. 672 (SE 24/34) - Harewood.

 - North Rigton - Almscliffe Crag - Cliff House - Holly Hill - North Rigton.

 - No official one.

- The Square & Compass Inn, North Rigton.

ABOUT THE WALK - I am totally biased about this gritstone outcrop, since I have been coming here for years; first from school on my bike. The crag is a visible landmark for miles around and I always enjoyed free-wheeling down Harewood hill with the crag in view. Here on Sunday's I sat under the rocks and waited for the offer of a rope and other times soled the hardest routes. It was here that I learnt to rock climb. This short walk takes you to the crag with ample time to wander around the "massif". You return over the fields back to North Rigton. There is car parking space on the west side of the crag, but I always feel it is better to walk there and see it beauty rather than park beside it!

WALKING INSTRUCTIONS - Starting from the road junction in North Rigton beside the Square and Compass Inn, ascend the road passing the inn on your right and in a few yards "High Fold". Just after turn left, as footpath signed - "Almscliffe Crag". The path crosses a field and soon becomes a lane that curves to your left to Crag Lane. At the lane on your left is your return path. Turn right and in a few yards right at a stile and path sign. The path is well stiled and you cross the fields towards Almscliffe Crag. Approaching the crag the path bears to the righthand side of it, but I always prefer to ascend to the crag's summit and wander around before descending a shallow easy gully to its base. Bear right to a stile and pick up the path again and at the end of the next field gain a stile, road and roadside parking spot.

- continued opposite.

SPOFFORTH & FOLLIFOOT - 4 1/2 MILES

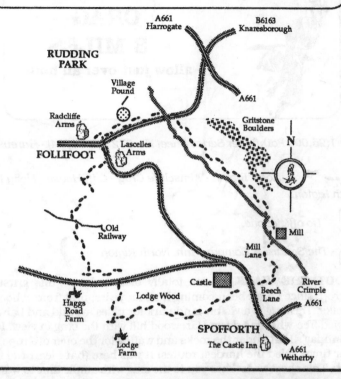

Cross over to your left and ascend the steps and continue along the field boundary on your left past a small wood to a gate and footpath sign almost opposite Haggs Road Farm. Turn left along Haggs Road and in 1/4 mile leave it, at a footpath sign on your right, and walk along a tarmaced drive towards Lodge Farm. You descend to Lodge Wood and stream and the other side of the wood turn left, as bridlepath signed, and walk beside the wood on your left. Pass through a gate and at the end of the next field cross a footbridge. Continue ahead ascending over the shoulder of a gorse covered slope, on a good path, and descend towards the old railway line. Adjacent to it you bear right then left through an archway and gain a small road. On your left is the castle. Continue to the main road beside Castle Field where you began.

SPOFFORTH CASTLE - The fortified manor house dates from the 14th century. Sir Henry Percy was granted permission to crenelate the house, but following his death in 1461, the house was savaged. In 1650 it was considerable dismantled.

SPOFFORTH & FOLLIFOOT
- 4 1/2 MILES
- allow 1 1/2 to 2 hours.

 1:25,000 Pathfinder Series Sheet No. 663 (SE 25/35) - Harrogate.

•◦ ◦• •◦ *- Spofforth - Mill Lane - River Crimple - Follifoot - Haggs Road Farm - Lodge Wood - Spofforth.*

- No official one. Roadside parking beside Castle Field - Grid Ref. 362512.

- The Castle Inn, Spofforth; Radcliffe Arms and Lascelles Arms, Follifoot.

ABOUT THE WALK - Another of my haunts! A really delightful walk, starting from Spofforth Castle. First past a former corn mill before walking along the banks of the River Crimple, with views of wind eroded boulders, like rock stacks in a sea of grass. Follifoot is an attractive village with a well preserved village pound (pinfold). You return over the fields with views to the Cleveland hills, with the White Horse on Roulston Scar clearly visible.

WALKING INSTRUCTIONS - From Castle Field, where the road turns left to the castle entrance, turn right along Beech Lane. At the road junction go straight across following Mill Lane to the mill. Leave the lane and pass the mill on its left to cross a footbridge before following the path beside the River Crimple on your left. The path is defined and well stiled. Keep beside the river for the next 1 1/2 miles to a minor road. Turn left along it and ascend to the village of Follifoot. Entering the village on your right is the village pound. Continue to the road junction in the village with the Rudding Gate (arch) on your right. Turn left along the road and just past the Post Office turn right, as footpath signed - "Haggs, Spofforth." The path meanders through the houses to a stile. Bear right over this and continue on a track, which soon curves left then right. Cross Horse Pond Beck and ascend with the hedge on your right. At the top turn right then left, still on a track, along the field boundary and descend to a former railway line.

- continued opposite.

NETHERBY AND THE RIVER WHARFE - 8 MILES

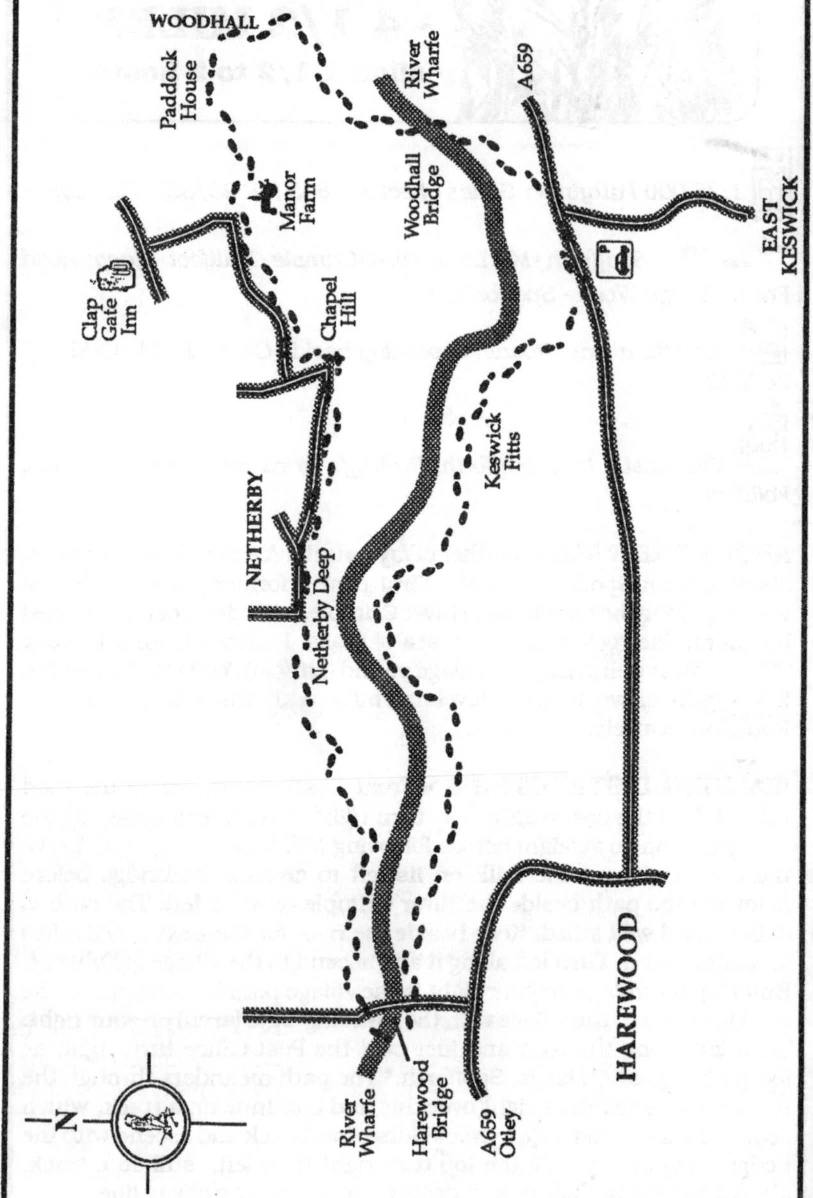

WOODHALL

Paddock House

Manor Farm

River Wharfe

A659

EAST KESWICK

Clap Gate Inn

Chapel Hill

Woodhall Bridge

NETHERBY

Netherby Deep

Keswick Fitts

River Wharfe

Harewood Bridge

A659 Otley

HAREWOOD

N

NETHERBY AND THE RIVER WHARFE - 8 MILES

- allow 3 hours.

1:25,000 Pathfinder Series Sheet No. 672 (SE 24/34) - Harewood.

🐾 - Car Park - A659 - River Wharfe - Keswick Fitts - Carthick Wood - Netherby Deep - Harewood Bridge - A61 - River Wharfe - Netherby - Chapel Hill - Manor Farm - Paddock House Farm - Woodhall Bridge - Car Park.

🚗 - Junction of the East Keswick road with the A659. Grid Reference 364454.

🍺 - None on the walk, but 1/4 mile off route is the Clap Gate Inn at Clap Gate. Another is in East Keswick.

ABOUT THE WALK - You encircle a segment of the River Wharfe; sometimes along its banks other times far from it, depending on the rights of way. Part of the route follows the Ebor Way. The river meanders through a wide valley with Harewood to the south.

WALKING INSTRUCTIONS - From the car park turn left along the A659 road towards Harewood, following the Ebor way to Netherby Deep. Pass the Lan-Den Nursery on your right and shortly afterwards on your right is the footpath sign. Turn right to a stile and gently descend down to the River Wharfe. You keep beside it a short distance before walking on the lefthand side of a wood at Keswick Fitts. After 1/4 mile your regain the river but leave it again briefly before walking through Carthick Wood. For the next 2 1/4 miles to Harewood Bridge you keep the river on your right as you keep close to the bankside on a good path. After 2 miles pass the base of a column on your left. Gaining the bridge and A61, turn right over it and immediately past the large building - a former school - turn right, as footpath signed. You follow a track which soon returns you to the river. After 1/2 mile follow the track away from the river and cross a ford. Continue to the left of a sewage plant and cross a bridge and keep on a track above the plant which swings to your right and becomes a hedged track.

At the end join a road at Netherby. Keep straight ahead past Mauston Caravan Park on your left and through the hamlet of Netherby. Follow the road round to your left and turn right along the minor road to Chapel Hill. In 1/2 mile the road turns sharp left around the hill. Just afterwards turn right along Gill Lane. To your left are great views to Almscliffe Crag and the river. Continue along the lane for a 1/3 mile to where it turns sharp left at Manor Farm for Clap Gate and Inn. Here leave the road keeping to the lefthand side of Manor Farm to a gate. Continue on a track before keeping the hedge and fence on your right as you cross the fields to the left of Paddock House Farm, 1/2 mile away. Gaining the farm road - Paddock House Lane - turn right along it passing Paddock House on your right. Keep on the tarmaced lane past West Plantation on your left and Old Wives Wood. At the second right turning go ahead to a gate, as footpath signed, and continue on a track towards the ground walls of Woodhall. Just before the wall turn right and descend the well used path - now back on the Ebor War - and reach Woodhall Bridge more than 1/4 mile away. Cross over and follow the track, first close to the river then ascending to the A659 road. Opposite is your car park.

EBOR WAY - is a 70 mile walk from Helmsley (The Cleveland Way) to Ilkley and the Dales Way.

River Wharfe and Harewood Bridge.

Spofforth Castle - Spofforth walk.

The Pound (Pinfold) - Follifoot - Spofforth walk.

HAREWOOD PARK
- 7 1/2 MILES

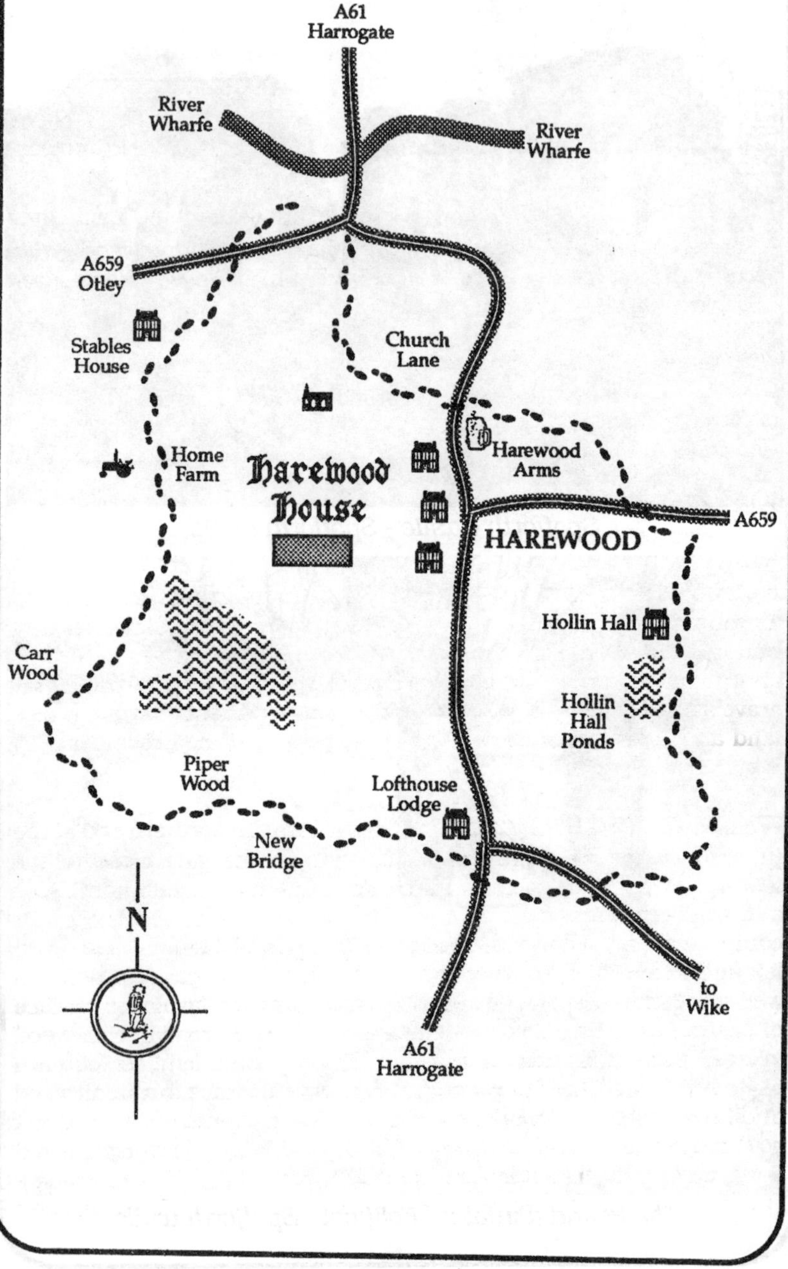

A61
Harrogate

River Wharfe

River Wharfe

A659
Otley

Stables House

Church Lane

Home Farm

Harewood House

Harewood Arms

HAREWOOD

A659

Hollin Hall

Carr Wood

Hollin Hall Ponds

Piper Wood

Lofthouse Lodge

New Bridge

N

to Wike

A61
Harrogate

HAREWOOD PARK
- 7 1/2 MILES
- allow 2 1/2 hours

 1:25,000 Pathfinder Series Sheet No. 672 (SE24/34) - Harewood.

- A61/A659 junction - North Park - Church - Church Lane - Harewood - A659 - New Laithe Farm - Hollin Hall - Spring Wood - Wike Wood - A61 - Lofthouse Lodge - New Bridge - Carr House - Home Farm - Stables' House Stud Farm - A659.

 - No official one. Road side parking near junction of A61/659 at Grid Ref. 313457. Layby on A659 near bridlepath to New Laithe Farm at Grid Ref. 335451. Roadside parking opposite Lofthouse Lodge at Grid Ref. 326432.

- Harewood Arms, Harewood.

ABOUT THE WALK - Harewood Hall is set in rolling countryside and as you walk round you get glimpses of this magnificent 18th century building. The village of Harewood was moved across the road but the church remains in situ and has a remarkable collection of 18th century grave stones. The walk encircles the parkland passing through woodland and following sections of the Ebor Way and the Leeds Country Way.

WALKING INSTRUCTIONS - Starting from the northern end at the junction of the A61/659 roads, go through the gate close to the footpath sign - "Church Lane" and begin ascending through North Park and beside woodland on your left, following a track. Gaining a gate continue ahead, ascending to a footpath sign and Church Lane. Turn left and immediately to your right is the path to the church, which is well worth the diversion to see. Continue along the tarmaced surface of Church Lane and follow it all the way to the A61 road in Harewood village. Turn right and almost immediately turn left, as footpath signed. in front of the Harewood Arms. Follow the track to a small wood and keep to the righthand side of it to a gate and onto another. Don't go through this one; instead turn right at a stile and walk along the field boundary to another stile and the A659 road. Turn left and in a few yards reach a layby and just after turn right, as bridlepath signed, and walk along the tarmaced road to New Laithe Farm. Walk around the lefthand side of it and continue on the track descending to a stream before ascending to Hollin Hall. Here as guided by signs walk around the lefthand side of it and gain the embankment of Hollin Hall Ponds. Just past the pond reach a gate and bear left beside Spring Wood on your left to another gate. Here continue ahead along the field edge with the fence/hedge on your left. After two fields reach another track - part of the Leeds Country Way - and turn right along the track, following it along past Wike Wood to a minor road. Turn right along it to its junction with the A61 road - small car parking space on your left.

Cross the A61 to the bridlepath through Harewood Park, passing Lofthouse Lodge on your right - you are still on the Leeds Country Way. The track at first is level and curves slightly to your right before descending, en route getting glimpses of Harewood House. The track descends to New Bridge. Here as guided by signs turn left then right, still keeping on a good track through Piper Wood. 1/4 mile later cross Stub House Beck and in just over 1/4 mile reach the junction with the Ebor Way. Turn right along it past Carr House and descend through Carr Wood to near the lake before ascending through Home Farm. The route is well signed. Cross cattle grids beyond the farm and gain a path junction. Here the Ebor Way turns right and you turn left then right and descend past Stables' House Stud Farm to the A659 road. Turn right back to the junction with the A61.

HAREWOOD HOUSE - Henry Lascelle bought the estate in 1738, which included Gawthorpe Hall; this was demolished in 1771. Edwin Lascelle built Harewood House in 1759 using stone from the estate and is reputed to have cost £100,000 and designed by John Carr of York. The grounds were laid out by Capability Brown in 1772.

New Bridge, Harewood Park.

Bishop Monkton - Bishop Monkton walk.

River Nidd and Knaresborough - Knaresborough walk.

WETHERBY
& INGMANTHORPE PARK
- 4 1/2 MILES

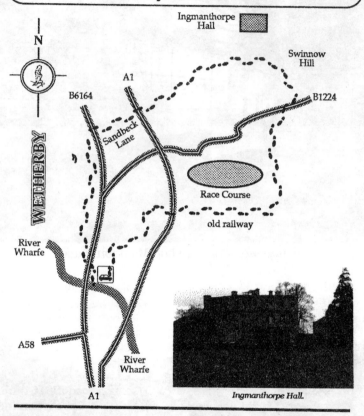

Ingmanthorpe Hall

Ingmanthorpe Hall.

N

B6164

A1

Sandbeck Lane

WETHERBY

River Wharfe

A58

River Wharfe

A1

Swinnow Hill

B1224

Race Course

old railway

to your right, and past a group of stables. Soon afterwards gain the railway bridge and turn right and descend to former track bed. Bear right along the old line and in just over 1/2 mile walk through a tunnel beneath the A1. Continue straight ahead along Freemans Way. At the road junction turn left along Hallfield Lane, passing a school on your right and as the lane turns right a cemetery on your left and Wetherby High School on your right. Continue to the end of the road and bear half left passing the covered market on your right. At the end of the road turn right passing the Fire Station on your left and descend the No Entry road, down to the car park and river.

WETHERBY - well worth exploring; especially around the Town Hall area.

WETHERBY
&
INGMANTHORPE
PARK
- 4 1/2 MILES
- allow 1 1/2 to 2 hours.

 - *1:25,000 Pathfinder Series Sheet No. 673 (SE 44/54) - Tadcaster.*

- Wetherby - Sandbeck Lane - Ingmanthorpe Park - Swinnow Park - Race Course - Old Railway Line - Wetherby.

 - *beside River Wharfe in Wetherby. Grid Ref. 404480.*

- Numerous in Wetherby. Passed are The George & Dragon, Red Lion, Crown Inn, The Brunswick and The Angel.

ABOUT THE WALK - A self indulgent one! A short walk retracing the steps I often took, walking from my school to Wetherby. The route passes my old school - Wennington School (Ingmanthorpe Hall), before gaining the York Road and Wetherby Race Course. You return along a former railway line and descend back to the River Wharfe and car park, where there is a picnic tables and riverside paths.

WALKING INSTRUCTIONS - Regain the main road (B6164) from the car park and turn right, walking along North Street. Continue ahead at the Y junction, still on the B6164 - Deighton Road. Just over 1/4 mile from the road junction turn right along Sandbeck Lane. Walk past the industrial units to the A1. Here take extreme care and cross over to the lane opposite. Walk along the lane passing Sandbeck Wood on your right and Sandbeck House on your left. Continue on the track which curves round to your right and in 1/4 mile joins the drive to Ingmanthorpe Hall. Continue along this and in another 1/4 mile, with the hall a field away on your left, turn right, as bridlepath signed, and follow the track round to a wood and to the drive to Swinnow Hill. Bear right, as signed, along the drive to the B1224 York Road.

Turn right and in a few yards left at the stile and footpath sign. Cross to the road and walk past the race course on your right, arena well to

- continued opposite -

WALK RECORD CHART

Date walked

BISHOP MONKTON & RIPON CANAL - 4 1/2 MILES ....

FOUNTAINS ABBEY - 4 1/2 MILES.................................

RIPLEY PARK & CASTLE - 4 1/2 MILES ....

BRIMHAM ROCKS - 7 1/2 MILES ....

KNARESBOROUGH & RIVER NIDD - 4 1/2 MILES ....

BEAVER DYKE RESERVOIRS - 8 MILES ....

PLUMPTON ROCKS - 6 1/2 MILES ....

ALMSCLIFFE CRAG - 3 MILES ....

SPOFFORTH & FOLLIFOOT - 4 1/2 MILES ....

NETHERBY & RIVER WHARFE - 8 MILES ....

HAREWOOD PARK - 7 1/2 MILES ....

WETHERBY & INGMANTHORPE HALL - 4 MILES ....

THE JOHN MERRILL WALK BADGE

Complete six of the walks in this book and get the above special badge and signed certificate. Badge are black cloth with lettering and walking man embroidered in four colours and measure - 3 1/2" in diameter.

BADGE ORDER FORM

Date and details of walks completed..

....

NAME ....

ADDRESS ....

....

Price: £3.00 each including postage, VAT and signed completion certificate.
Amount enclosed (Payable to El Morro Equipment Ltd) ..

From: El Morro Equipment Ltd.,
19, Moseley Street, Ripley,
Derbyshire. DE5 3DA

© /Fax (01773) - 512143 - 24hr answering service.
********** *YOU MAY PHOTOCOPY THIS FORM* ***********

"I'VE DONE A JOHN MERRILL WALK" T SHIRT

- Green with white lettering and walking man logo.
Send £7.50 to El Morro Equipment Ltd., stating size required.
John Merrill's "Happy Walking!" Cap - £3.00

"From footprint to finished book"